"Life is not death" and if you walk with Alexej Savreux's Moonshine Ethics For a New Humanity, this will seep into your bloodstream slowly and surely—or, rather, maybe like a cold, Southern sweet tea chugged on a hot, July day. In any case, Savreux's poems take pleasure in mixing things up for a nice spin: philosophical adages, questions, observations, and life situations weaved to unstrap our lives from the weary and mundane. An amalgamation of styles, lexicon, narratives, and allusions to whistle a soft, drifting love through life that might even be a cosmic exhalation of Philia. Or a holding of hands with Agape.

—Timothy Dodd, author of *Galaxy Drip* (Luchador Press) and *Vital Decay* (Cajun Mutt Press)

"Moonshine Ethics For a New Humanity, blesses one in its confessions, informs in its reflections, warms us in its satire, and disarms and embraces in its sincerity. Alexej Savreux talks directly and unflinchingly to the human condition, in a collage of aphorism, micro-dialogues, epistles, pleadings, lyrical flights, and stream-of-conscious sketches. Alexej reminds us, "life wouldn't be fun if it weren't so damn complicated." Isn't that the truth. I'll keep this book close and remember always it sits alongside Antonio Porchia's Voices and Marcus Aurelias's Meditations."

-Jose Faus, Artist, poet, activist

"Alexej Savreux's work is a love poem to an "odd, odd, odd world" and all who inhabit it. In poems that can be terse or expansive, he reminds us that "Humanity is where Hope is". He can be intimate and obsessive, like a long coffee-fueled confab with a close friend after a night of moonshine. Always thinking, full of hopeful possibilities, he gives us a cure for the hangover of our times."

-Eric Rensberger, *Notes to Self*
(Stubborn Mule Press, 2025)

"In Moonshine Ethics for a New Humanity, Alexej Savreux unleashes poems that serve as both a reckoning and a celebration—a neon-lit odyssey from a poet who values the overlooked and mourns the dwindling rarity of unfiltered authenticity. With deftness, he creates moments of straightforward salve: "Be calm and be genuine, thank you, and I love you too." Whether reflecting on capitalism's failings, offering direct assessments of everyday life, or exploring the baffling nature of our minds' wild workings, Savreux writes with a broad sensibility that carries on the legacy of Bill Knott. And the world is better for it."

-Jordan Stempleman, *Cover Songs*
(The Blue Turn, 2022)

Moonshine Ethics
For a New Humanity

Poems by Alexej Savreux

Spartan
Press

Spartan Press

Kansas City, Missouri

Spartan
Press

Copyright © Alexej Savreux, 2025

First Edition: 1 3 5 7 9 10 8 6 4 2

ISBN: 978-1-958182-77-2

LCCN: 2024950502

Cover image: Smeza

Author photo: Talia H.

Several of these poems have appeared elsewhere throughout the last few years: "BeAt ThA DUh" appeared in the *Writers Place Yearbook: An Anthology of Writing by Writers Place Members,* 2023. "Glaucon, Revisited," "A Series of Japanese Techniques to Make Life Better," and "Eating Korean Pork & Kimchi & Rice at Christmas in the End Times" appeared in *The Gasconade Review Presents: No One Sees the Irony* from OAC Press in 2024.

"Homily," "Be Sure to Know the Names of Your Flowers Before Your Garden is Gone," as well as several other philosophical-poetical pieces were self-published in various forms over the years or took the form of calligraffiti and graffiti in different places and on multiple windows and walls in community colleges, art studios, whiteboards, and in alleys in Jackson, and Wyandotte counties from 2017 to 2024.

As always, I am indebted to Jason Ryberg for helping bring this project to life, and I thank him for his editorial input in this process—also, Spartan Press and the folks at Prospero's Bookstore. I want to thank and acknowledge my dear friends Jose Faus and Dee Jimenez aka MC Sorcerer of Kaczynski Composite Sketch, for their unflagging personal and professional support and for some of the richest friendships of my life. I also want to acknowledge Maria Vasquez Boyd, CGP, my Mom, & SUNY Oneonta, Garry Noland, Craig Auge, Cathy Schrag, the Stojanovic family (every last one of them), my Gram, Tom P & fam, Smeza, Crystle, CB, Tyler, KUMC's Addiction Clinic, Sarah Hornung, Teresa aka Riri Lara, Mike Sanders, Nick Christman, the KCMO & KCK arts scenes, and the entire Sanchez family for reasons that require no elaboration here.

It is difficult for me to imagine ever topping the crop of people I have in my life. And I sing my highest praises, love, and thanks to all, whether expressed here specifically or not.

Table of Contents

"…do not weep; life is paradise, and we are all in paradise, but we do not want to know it, and if we did want to know it, tomorrow there would be paradise the world over."

~ The Brothers Karamazov

This book is for the dear memory of both Steph
and my father, Brian

~ Ad Astra Per Aspera ~

Moonshine Ethics
For a New Humanity

Homily

People too often say things like:

"Love is the most mysterious, most inexplicable of all
phenomena."

But Love was never a mystery to me

Love is not "I can't live without you." Love is:

"Your happiness, health, and prosperity are my
happiness, health, and prosperity."

Jealousy and possessiveness kill Love

Love is selflessness

True Freedom is Found only in Love

Sept. 12 2019

- transcribed by Grace G

A year ago I was asked, "what do you care about?" After thinking it over, I replied, "Creating & sharing ideas, helping people, & cultivating friendships & relationships. And beyond that, virtually nothing else matters to me." Today, & 50 years from now, I won't change a damn word.

Colorado '07-'08 (in bits)

I favor the Sonnet, Love!
 Ah, shared with me...from isles hast depart, I await;
And lead thither Raphael and the Archangels
 To speak of Wisdom;
Of thee and thyne O, every Heart has been my Home
All my life has been my Prayer
Love was one
 And life was won
Frozen young;
 A Black Sea where yesterday is dangling
And facing the changing times
 The year's Brought us to our knees;
Regret what? Blah! Meh! He doesn't regret a thing
Pure poetry breathes pure and beautiful life!
 "We're never going to die!" Said Alexej in 2003;
 Exhaling a big hit'o weed
"Why?" Asked Tina, his friend's fleshed angel
Painted the forlorn pastures of our settlement;
We are timeless spoken words upon the yielded knees and
 needs
60 or 70 + years aeterna
And beyond What?
HA! We get back in the pickup truck - the hours is approaching
 potsmoke time and cigarettes, and probably taco bell, and
 drunkenness in the morning after night . . .
 I'M THE MAN IN THE BOX!!!
Freedom down the Coloraad-O freeway forever and e'er
 headed down South

Some Emotions Serve No Purpose

I think the best revenge in life (if one chooses actually to call it "revenge") is getting to a place in life where one doesn't even feel like revenge is necessary

Be Sure to Know the Names of Your Flowers Before Your Garden is Gone

Full of joy be that day
When from the ashes shall arise
New flower to be plucked;
Therefore spare dirt, O God,
Merciful Lord,
Grant petals eternal peace. Amen.

A Poem That Most of You will Forget By Noon But I Hope Not

Anger and pessimism are emotions

Unfettered gratitude is a flower that never stops blooming

Bethany

Been thinking about you

Hanging out in my small Kansas City, Kansas house, that
fun, dope sublet in the student ghetto back before
the moonshine times

I been thinking about your big, beautiful smile and laugh,
sitting on the stoop drinking 40 oz watermelon iced
tea in the cool autumn morning mist

Going for walks around the neighborhood - fall '17

I hope you don't stay jaded by the world or by things,

I know it's been a rough life, but I would hate to hear it
ever consumed you

Please know there aren't any hard feelings

You did what you had to do, but still, I often find myself
asking: if even you would reject me, what can I
possibly hope for from anyone else?

Part of me died in 2023

You kept me alive, and you killed me, and still, I am an',
so I hafta come back to life again, ha!

"If I ever break you, just tell me so that way I can put you
back together again!" - you used to say; it used to make
me feel whole again;

I came to know life and affection back in the good ol' days—
and I've never stopped feeling treasured by you

I been thinking about it, and thinking about you - and I
choose to remember it for what it was, and I'm hanging
my head in fondness and mystery

Because that's what those 6 1/2 years were --- immense

What am I supposed to do? Hate you for loving me?

I smile when I think of it all and smile when I think of you

Life has a way of happening.

And still, here I am

Untitled but Apropos

If you stare into a blackhole long enough, eventually
(perhaps with the right set of eyes) you'll see right through
it and marvel at the other side of the universe

An SMS Text After Hugo in Yet Another Emergency Room

Love you Dad. You can do it. Even the darkest night will end and the sun will rise.

Hindu-Buddhist Folk Sing A-Long

Let me put some wisdom on you
Lemme spit some wisdom down in you;

Love your people.
Cuz you know what? At the end of the day and the end
    of all other things and when all is said and when all
    is done, loving your people and each other is all that
    ever is was or will or even could be;
So be thankful,
And stay connected to the Earth beneath your feet

Ah, then Let us Sip Something Cold to Drink
aka Rejoyce

another year around the sun,
another round of heartbeats for everyone, and well,
    yesterday, I was 30, just turned 31
then I was 32, 33, 34, and suddenly 35 and almost closer
    to 40 than 30!
A new plague? After the last new plague?
What plagues humans?
The loss of time? The befuddlement of chaos?
Chasing dreams obliterated by societal nihilism
cloistered and sunken;
lost, beat, blank, broke?
post-post-post-modern?
I miss working at Jimmy John's
and I miss big sis;
I miss being a kid even in the before times - it's not just
    five years I've seen gone by;
it took me 20+ years to recover the grand prize, the prize
    of a lifetime
the revocation of blundered redeemably dense
    potheadian lunacy
and here I sit, young middle-aged now, and half broken
    but forever grateful, forever happy and at peace,
it feels like all my life, I've watched the world through a
    window
each day indistinguishable from the next
carried off into the midnight hours in the back of an
    ambulance
put in chemical restraints

force-fed benzos and muscle relaxants, and neuroleptics and
    anticonvulsants
we have the present and the future
the past can't be unwritten, and the past can't be undone
so what?
Do we wait?
I used to trade food in the psych wards like in prison, ha!
I'd get two pieces of cake for some tomato soup or both!
Maybe a Code Red Mountain Dew if I was lucky enough
So there! What?
There's nothing profound about it all... make the best of your
    time and what means
something special to you
I miss those wards of oblivion
I miss a lot of things
but no time is wasted unless you don't enjoy wasting it
ah, the gift of youth ala Russell
so behold, the purpose and meaning of life;
different definitions from sages and academics and thinkers
    and poets;
My answer? Well, I suppose if I had to provide one, I'd be
    grateful for the bizarreness of my life and my weird
    journey and pursuit of self-actualization
it never gets boring
and I never lose hope
Hope is an ancient spiritual principle
and that is worth noting
remember, there is an art to experience
and I think life wouldn't be fun if it weren't so goddamn
    complicated

Deathical

when I die many, many years from now
I assure you they'll find me with a couple of bottles of
    Diet Mountain Dew
some books, some CDs, and cassettes, and I don't know
    maybe some Thai Food or a
few Minsky's pizza boxes with poetry and jokes scribbled
    on them in sharpie ink,
maybe a couple of cartons of American Spirit menthol
    lights, or Camels, and a gigantic,
fucking smile on my face
Life is not death

Ism Ism Ism

We talk about capitalism - is it slavery?
Well, clinically feudalism, slavery, and capitalism, where you
    have the masters and
lords and those who control the power and wealth as a tiny
    minority and those who do
the bulk of the work (aka the majority) for little to no
    money or with no fighting
chance; then yes
The big talk of the town is capitalism and socialism
but nobody knows what either is, despite what they like to
    claim
they say they're Marxists or communists or Marxist-
    Leninists
Peeps know this iteration of capitalism isn't working on
    both sides
So they lay claim to socialism…ism-ism-ism-ism-ism.
people want affordable healthcare, a living wage, a
    functional economy, environmental
action, democratization,
affordable housing, and no predatory lending.
that isn't Marxism, communism, or socialism in any
    scientific sense
they're just good ideas
ism-ism-ism-ism-ism
eliminate the "-isms," O academics!
let's dish about good ideas in the moonshine times o'er a
    sweet elixir n' the mizzuruh moon
o'er the railroads in KCK, let's go further rural
out east in between KCMO and ol' St Lou

just sit round a fire, eat some chicken, maybe fried
    chicken, and talk good ideas
You can be anyone like Johnny Rotten, who is going over
    the Berlin Wall and suddenly
chanting, "Build the wall!"
All I ask of anyone is that they be genuine and they be
    sincere
the moonshine of our time is the power of our inner
    loveliness
a sweet elixir on a 1 dimensional plane or a 2-dimensional
    object round in circles like
a scratchy vinyl record on repeat
the same banal absurdities
Douglas Adams would be so entertaining in the
    moonshine times
But let yourself fall backward into the grassy grass with a
    bottle of moonshine, stare up
at those Mizzuru stars, and get your eyes off your
    ideological feet.
Here, have a chicken wing; they're delightful!

On Whorf's Analysis of Psychology

Psychology is a remarkably intuitive and tautological
    discipline
Whorf had that 110% correct in some of his writings ("On
    Psychology" (an essay)
I don't view human behavior or anything in the biosciences
    or psychoanalysis or
philosophy or existentialism as being particularly complex,
    but then again, sometimes
the simplest things are the most complex and the most
    complex things quite simplex:
        Most everything, from human behavior to
    gravitation, is about connection
People aren't so complicated. Even the most "depraved"
    (as society calls them) it's
merely a desire for a greater connection, communion to a
    primary human emotional
and spiritual need;
Shit…even gravitation is about attraction
I honestly, intellectually believe that everything in the universe
    is just on a perpetual
cosmic quest to get laid. Uhhh..who said that? Shakespeare?

Untitled Bit

Another year gone by is not time lost, but 'tis time gained

Weird Family Backstory, I Guess

My whole existence is everywhere and nowhere

The Power of Poverty

My political views are often misunderstood in light of
    the ongoing culture wars
            lots of amorphous overlapping spheres
Really politically I'm like Paul Erdos — I'd like to just go
    from Poland to Kansas to UCLA
to Delaware to New York to Princeton doing nothing
    except writing, creating,
speaking, collaborating; research, publish, work and
    social practice
            I don't want anything more than two backpacks
    worth of stuff
No more than two square meals a day like chicken wings
    or taco bell
Maybe a cot or sleep on the floor in a sleeping bag in a
    dingy basement
                    I'm one of the few people I've known
Who says let me die poor
I want to die poor
Because money doesn't make me rich or full; I don't
    have them kinda riches!
I want to die full of life and a life well lived
            it's the people, really the little people that make
    life count, like you Griswold!

Pale Blue Dot of Splendour

What does it mean to be an artist or a poet?
It means you, therefore, love all humanity
And consent to compassion;
> there is an inherent need for compassion in the
> world
—— compassion without deference,
> whereby we recognize each other's shortcomings,
> faults, and limitations as
being the byproduct of our unique but universalized
> struggles to navigate the shoals
of life and thus granting grace to others with an aim for
> contemplation and a brave
submission to the whims of existence;
> and yet no solace found in unpleasance, but we
> can perhaps find solace
In knowing there exists for all of us, the pressures of pain
> and the satieties of pleasure
> and the odd, odd, odd, world in which
> we have found ourselves
And our fundamental, even primal need for acceptance;
> our respective weirdnesses
intimated through conversation and art, the part
> unacknowledged or unwilling to
present themselves to the world therefore, tapped, and
> goodness reigns instead of the
bad stuff. We see each other as we are; as children, adults,
> older men or women,
before and after, existence and obliteration, birth, life,
death, the three and one

miraculous totality, with the artist's eyes, and the poet's
moods, we examine the sappy
loveliness, always expanding and contracting with the
    pulsating power of loftier
promises within controlled chaos. No love is ever thus
    totally demolished; it grows and
grows and yet grows more;

And there is no defeat in that
        There is but peace and there is but power

Reflection I

It's important to remember that every season of life is
good
I'm not saying travesties don't happen or that
living isn't difficult
I'm not saying you aren't allowed to feel because you most
definitely are allowed to feel
I'm not imploring you not to try to
make sense of the pieces of the puzzle
of the past
It's okay to have regrets or reminisce on youth or other
phases
It's also essential we recognize we can struggle, and that's
okay, too
I've come to realize there is beauty in birth and death and
everything in between
but it's critical to remember that so much isn't
up to you or really up to any one
person; the fate or trajectory of the universe is not a
weight any one person or group
can shoulder; that's not on you; that is up to a higher
power, er, something akin to
that; whatever one wants to call it is their business,
beeswax, etc
it's just the arbitrariness of the universe
- so much of what happens in
the universe is actually just random
But, as helpless as we might sometimes be,
and as insignificant as we all are (or otherwise
might feel), it is vital to keep in
mind — we do have each other

Life is the Beatific Vision

I sail as music through a universe of infinities
              where, like a ghost, I keep company with
 laments and glowing Angels

Reflection II

Knowing that you will one day die should remove the
  fear of taking a risk to pursue
something or someone you love, even if that something
  might seem insignificant to
others. Life is not a spectator sport. By trying, even if
  you fail, you are still succeeding
in another way. To be alive is one thing, but to live is
  something else entirely.

Kasparov Gets an MFA

There once was an eccentric kid with a
Stocking hat and thick, messy hair
He had a fondness for linguistics mathematics and art,
He used to wander around KCMO on his feet
At least 5 miles every day, probably more like 10 miles
(And nights) on the streets
        He worked at Jimmy John's & his favorite
    sandwiches were the
Veggie and the Club Tuna (although now he prefers
    something with turkey and bacon
or the chicken protein wraps with aioli and stuff)
He likes almond milk decaf lattes at Opera House
For awhile, he worked as a computational linguist
    fighting off the AI data models in math and language
He is currently an MFA student
His nickname is the linguistics delinquent
He is paradoxical, like an eccentric comic book-reading
    savant
His friend said his new poetry book should be called
"Kasparov Gets an MFA."
He is considering this title
        And now he just finished a poem about it and
    will wait to see how many "likes" he gets
He also likes STEAM and satire, especially Lenny Bruce
    and social theory
His favorite social theorist is R.D. Laing
Obviously, he likes Foucault as well
And he loves you

Reflection III (From a Panel Discussion at Cleveland University in May 2019)

I believe that in History, failure is never final
Provided it is not accepted as final
So if all seems lost, void, or altogether hopeless
I would impress upon you the natural adaptability
And resiliency each of you possesses
Because life causes suffering
And you cannot escape suffering
But I assure you you are equal to the task
So keep going
Keep trying
Because life is not a static endpoint
It is a fluid and dynamic process
And life doesn't happen to you
Life happens for you
Life is a Gift
Enjoy it

Starshine

I refuse to see the sky as anything but lit by billions and billions and billions of radiant Suns.

Entropy (a thing shall begin a-new)

All those ships that never sailed
Prayers and Peace
      and rest thine head in the cottage of dusk

Adaptation

I am tired
Writing on the walls of my ancestors
Way back
      the wise man emerged

Graffiti on the Berlin Wall

The grave leaves plenty of time for silence
Go be heard, man

A Brief Belief About Human Goodness

Heart see here — as a water balloon
Tasked as the rain;
          filled with the Christened water
Of Joy
Ah, & upon Death;
 The bulbous balloon explodes
The affectionate water flows like a cosmic faithful
Ocean, becoming the face of pure Love itself;

Faith as a Friend & Spiritual Principle

My therapist told me to write a poem about my best friend,
    so I wrote a one-line poem
about you, and I think you change
    the world. It's sort of a pun and also metaphorical.
Would you like to hear it?

"Faith is what gives the world hope."

Is that it?

Yep, straight from my heart BFF

I love it!

Reflection IV

One of the most beautiful things about love is that it doesn't require constant gratitude.

Bodhisattva (Mic Check, 1 and 2,
Mic Check 1 and yeah . . .)

Someone loves me, and I love them
Someone hates me, and I love them
Someone yells at me, and I love them
Someone abuses me, and I love them
Someone gets angry, and I love them
Someone lies to me, and I love them
Someone steals from me, and I love them
Someone cheats or gossips, and I love them
Someone wrongs me or others, and I love them
And someone learns to love and grow, and I love them

A Series of Japanese Techniques to
Make Life Better

To discover one's purpose in life?

        determine the reason you wake up each
   morning; choose that which aligns with
your strengths, embodies your values and passions, and is
   something the world needs
Focus on minor improvements every day
        nothing significant or major; just little things
Take breaks if you're stressed or being overly productive,
   walk away, and then come
back to it after a bit of a respite;
Eat until you're about 70-80% full (something that has
   long been said to be a key to longevity)
        What did they once say?
For we never repent of having eaten too little?
The beginner's mind is the Master's mind; therefore,
   approach as a beginner in everything you do
        and embrace imperfection! Perfection doesn't
   exist, and
done is, therefore (and likewise), far better than "perfect."
  Spend time in nature for a good portion of the day.
   One needs nature but does not
need technology. Fuck technology. The Industrial
   Revolution and its consequences
have been a disaster for the human race
        live within your means; frugality is ideal;

Aha! Peace to You, my Eternal Friend, Ag'en!

We'll spread your ashes in the Gulf of Mexico!
Here's a shot of whiskey—remember to always dream big,
    dream of something, and
never stop dreamin', boys. Ah-a!

HUZZAH!!

To life! (**cheers**) —- "TO LIFE!" (**boisterous applause**)

BeAt ThA DUh

Never had a country
I've never had a Home;
I have no ideology
And I'm tired of dealing with Bioooolooogy
Anyways, the thing is, what I really mean:
My life and my work are sui generis
And those eyes are gypsy, gypsy eyes;
I hope someone doesn't mind; I hope you don't mind
That I put down in words
How wonderful life is when people take like half a step back
Get back get back get back to where they always belonged
He got burnt jamb eyeballs and Holy Thank Yous inspired
    by high art gratitude
            below his knees;
Got to be yourself cuz there's nothing else to BE
Come Together! RIGHTTTTTT NOW!
                    cuz the people need peace
            (primarily of mind)
The media industrial complex system and its consequences
    have been a disaster for
the human race
Life's a Bath
Satori is Water

Ahhhh uhh....aughhh!!

My Father Smokes a Pipe in a Toyota SUV

My father smokes a pipe full of tobacco in a Toyota SUV
        barreling thru the NY countryside into Vermont
Foggy;
        It's cold; his arthritis has been getting the poor guy
But as much as I used to feel alienated, there's something
    poignant and comforting
        perhaps even comfortable about a 72-year-old
    man with scoliosis smoking a
pipe in a Toyota, an Americanized Serb
            Puffing, Puffing, Puffing,
  Christmas soon. Colder than fuck. NY winters
        Coffee at a Stewart's
Woods and forests everywhere
My God!
        Being a schizoid is too easy
And I fucking love most every minute of it

Satieties

Transience is beautiful, and transience is painful
        there is life; there is death, and there is eminent
    reality in both;

                    ah, such implacable slander against
    the great hand of effort and time; of
trial and tribulation; the pacifist ridding the worst in us
    and riding a Horse calling out
for redemption and redemption; still

The Frontiers of Empiricism Have Failed Us

The failures of science are immense.
        In Science's most brilliant and ebullient moments,
    it provides a how or a means
or explanation, maybe a pitiful or poor one, an irrational
    attempt at the
unknowingness of the all-encompassing eternity and
    "ever-is" cosmos
     buuuut "why"?
        unusual questions are often answered by people,
     by art and by
    literature; by creativity; by
humor; by relationships, friendships; romance; family;
    adventure, and the art of
experience; the rich feelings and emotions contained within
    thought, expression, and
mystery…and a keenly lived life — which cannot be
    described with the clarity of
mathematics, yet we often either find clarity without
    meaning or meaning without
clarity or sometimes we find both and realize we still have
    neither;
        But the unknowingness bathing our
    brains in the bathtub of philosophy
forever and ever, asking why and finding answers as rich as
    our best, shining brightest
experiences; that's all there is, was, and ever will be, and the
    world is all the better for
its very unknowingness if we and when we should choose
    to remember:
      'we don't always know'

I am Grateful for Grief (But Life Can Still be a Motherfucker)

Oh geez, I remember sitting in IOP group therapy in Kansas
    "I would rather die with a broken heart than live
    with one."
Said an older woman of her daughter's suicide
  heartwrenching, indeed it was to all in the room
Aside from that, my ADHD maggot brain pharmaceutical
    industry complexed out
Poetically, remembering complex traumas and many things
Principles of life: without death, no life; without sadness, no
    joy; without conflict, no
peace - this world is many things. A utopia of the literature
    wouldn't be particularly desirable…
        The world is already entirely utopian with all the
    people and things in it
And I hope people whose eyes read these lines can see these
    things sometime in their lives:
  For flowers bloom, the Sun rises, the Sun sets, children are
    born, people go through
the various phases of life, people make good art, young girls
    smile, people date;
Boys play baseball, football, and hockey
Teenagers go to the movies; the seasons change, the storms
    come and go;
        People fall in Love, they break up, divorce, but still
    others get married
They live and love together; life is a beautiful fucking mess.
    And in that way, it's
already such a perfectly imperfect utopia. Aha!

And so I politely and delicately ask all who suffer (and that
therefore includes all of humanity):
What suffering is not a gift from the gods?

Rest brings sleep, and tomorrow is a new day
And with it, infinite potentialities and a fresher Heart
rejuvenated
Tomorrow brings with it an increased perspective
And behold, the beauty of the present and all presents and
presence
We can always learn to live and experience life more keenly
And for that, we should be grateful
in the grateful, we emphasize the purest blissful
contentment
With grandest optimistic hearts a-beating not far behind

Nietzsche Was a Simpleton

There is more God in psych wards than in most other places on this Earth. People of all different backgrounds and creeds, barely hanging on — against the unrelenting weight of institutions and odds, against the crushing weight of ill health and against addiction and pain; the hostile brothels of despair, barely hanging onto the world of the living when most others see well, - nothing, beseeching the cosmos for respite, and solace, anything approaching equanimity — yes, there is far more life and certitude in the destitute, the poor, the forgotten, the lunatics, — in those wards of oblivion than there is in most any suburban Church I've ever entered.

It's where all forms of academic philosophy as any physician or PhD or PsyD could understand it is inverted and begins to break down unsystematically. The wards are where you meet God or whatever the hell you want to call it — from all different angles and confront and absorb the utterly existential, and veil it hence in inscrutable humor few others will ever be able to understand, or decipher - no matter their degree of learnedness or whatever their I.Q. happens to be; some humor and optimism are reserved for those who know too much about pain, shrouded in unusual gratitude late at night near the vending machines in the hospital cafeteria — I'll give you my ice cream sandwich for your chocolate milks, dude, cool, yeah?

Be Thoughtful

I used to believe that people died from suicide, but now
    I think that's specious logic
People don't die from suicide
They die from exhaustion
They die from confusion
They die from broken Hearts
They die from things they can't unsee
They die from trauma
They die from disease and addiction
They die from sadnesses
They die from desperation
They die from poverty
They die from not being heard
And they die from having difficulty navigating our overly
    bureaucratic, unnecessarily
complicated healthcare system.
And I in no way am equating the two with not going for
    life; we must always choose life.
For as far as we know, life is preferable to death
But the way I've described it is perhaps a humane way of
    discussing matters that aren't
simple, and which are in no way, - hyperboles
They are serious, solemn matters that demand the
continuous adaptation of all of our common affections
    and attention;
I hope all such people can rest in the peace they so rightly
    deserved

French to English Sight, in Extempore

Rain falls softly on the city.

I am Excited For You

I hope the troubles of our time affords you proper hope;
        provides said hope, for in chaos, nature makes
   peace with itself ag'en and ag'en
  In disorder or chaos, there is the potential for goodness
   and righteousness
  It is corroborated by human history

Marooned

Life is a Sea
While we Live, we Sail, we Float, and Swim, and churn
and flail and tread
       and Dream
Eventually, we all drown

y'all eat well & look after yrselves now

For those who lost the will to fight, rest easy
For those struggling to hold on, keep faith
The world is a better place with you in it

Kick it to the Moonshine

There are ever so many reasons to remain optimistic in the
    moonshine era;
        the political system is fucked, and any sensible
    sociopolitical commentary is ignored;
But there is still fundamental goodness:
        People are trying, and life is pretty fucking good
             they are merely trying to live their lives
    with a bit of hope and dignity
  Per Michael J Fox: "With gratitude, optimism is sustainable."
I'm betting the 2020s are far more insane than insane itself,
    But by the 2030s, things
will quiet back down again to boring, inane, centrist serenity
I'm not hoping for a centrist future
Neo-liberalism bent to the left or right (only in social
    scenarios) is dead
And I fear sparsity…I fear the dream of universal liberal
    democracy is dead, and the
moment for a genuine socialist program has come and gone;
            what is left seems to be either eco-
    anarchism derivative of Dr. Theodore
J. Kaczynski (minus the violence and domestic terrorism, of
    course) and various French
anarchists sympathetic to that sort of philosophical
    arrangement and historical evolution
        and potentially a kind of cyber-libertarianism or
    the French, le cyber libertaire!
Maybe HST-style left-wing libertarianism
Or a kind of social democratic experiment
Hope is never lost, not even in the moonshine era

For the ethics are redeemed in the loveliness of action,
	action, action, and still more action!
			As Mao? Said something akin to where
There is chaos, there is opportunity
				leave each other alone
No wars, no intervention (except humanitarian, of course)
Freedom for all colonized peoples
The political and psychological legacy of dominant society
	thinking needs to die a
brutally agonizing, inglorious, painfully fast, and unforgiving
	death
And then the technicalities of the technological system
Can benefit all of humanity and not just a select
OF or BY or FOR has never come to pass. And that is the
	great sadness.
			Humanity is where Hope is
For all one needs to have hope and great fortune is to hope;
	Then gratitude and optimism and a wonderful life splays
		open like a radiant, sunlit
flower unlike any beauteous specimen
	Any homo sapien could ever possibly have laid eyes on
A little insect just existing in Oregon or Southern Vermont
				suddenly becomes a Sage
And cooperation found in nature
In our past preludes the righteousness of rescue; the human
	Legacy is Love

Writ on My 31st Birthday Morn - Feb 8th, 2020

It is true that to be a light, you must be willing to let
    yourself burn
But it is also true that to be a-light
You merely have to be the opposite of heavy
So? Asks the painter

 Par consequent! Life is joie de vivre
And that is all anyone ever needs to get!

I Ain't Got Them Kinda Riches!

In 2018, I took to prophecy
I wrote a poem called "Ode 2 God."
I dished on how a world with nothing but me and my
    heart
And other people, and their hearts made me
Richer than $$$$$$ could
I watch the KC skyline at dawn every day 2 this day
My heart feels like a water balloon
Niagra Falls, the water floods my heart, but my heart
It just gets bigger and bigger every second I'm alive
Madly in Love Burning with Love
For everyone and everything

So ah!
        L-I-F-E !!
And yet, it won't pop
 My heart Ain't no popcorn kernel
The prophecy is TRUE!

My whole body burns for the world
  Except for my heart, which does not take a flame!

Aha! I am the richest person I have yet to meet
        and years later, NO THING I possess except
  Love and peace
O beautiful, sad young world

Good luck putting a price tag on people's hearts

      You feel me, everyone?!

  Haha YEA!!

The Ostracized Saint

The ostracized saint spread his arms
See here; this is how much I love you
The forgotten, the bereft, the marginalized
If it be in the icy silence of the womb
Or so by the moon's melodious light
May birth again
  Though thou be deaf and mute
And blind, but see now
 My arms — I hold them toward you.

A Stoned Analytic Philosopher is a Stoned Analytic Philosopher, While a Stoned Continental Philosopher is a Poet

My philosopher friend told me I wasn't a real philosopher
  I told him I was a Poet,
And therefore as good as any Continental Philosopher
who smokes a ton of weed
    His snarky smirk eroded

Gigs & Some Comments

1.

Springsteen hits all the hearts of young men working at warehouses and washing dishes—men with no direction, waiting on next week's paycheck. A young man needs a father.

2.

I hadn't heard this song in at least 23 years until today. And I sang it word for word. Nothing on earth is like music.

E-mail to a French-American Psychoanalyst Amid Plague

To H. Claude,

At some point, I will obviously have to come back, even
    if my intent is to move back east later.
Part of me is so "unused" to having a warm, fresh bed, a
    house, seemingly endless
food, home-cooked meals, company, a town to walk around
    in, a change of scenery, a
backyard, family, nice little uncrowded restaurants etc, that
    I don't quite feel "ready" to leave.
There is a little boy inside me, Claude, who, for whatever
    reason, was traumatized very
early on, and I can't quite figure out "why" – on bad days,
    I'm overcome with migraine
attacks and visions, tics, and debilitating fear. There is also
    tearfulness and stress, and
insomnia for reasons I can't identify or at the very least
    physiological mechanisms I
can't currently articulate.
I'm not going to lie. My nerves and numbness are one big
    central nervous system
shitstorm at the moment.
Immediate plans to return to KCMO will be revived once
    my stress quiets down a bit
It may sound neurotic, but I glanced at the headlines last
    night, and it feels like I'm
living in a poorly-written stoner Ray Bradbury novel.
It's also combined with elements of Douglas Adams, only
    not funny, and Soviet

propaganda about the evils of capitalism from the 1970s
At least I haven't lost my sense of humor
Yes, please get back to me when you can.
I hope this all makes sense.

Always the best,

A Savreux

Beyond the Dagger of Macbeth

Love is what makes things real

Window of a Pariah

Cruising at 30,000 feet
Confused because everyone else continues to argue
about where to travel

Open Letter to the World - Jan 31, 2021

Even 4 all its horrors ppl do wonders w/ life
Children are thrilled by harmless terror
And feeling good comes after strife
Peace of mind follows the deluge
I will always love you. I will find you.

<3 A.S.

Ha, it Reminds me of an Old Joke, you know!

The circus for Lacan is always in town.
The objet petit may not be a circus qua circus but it requires
    a clown
The clown here is not Alexej per se but rather capitalism
    which cannot exist without
commodification of the satirist and so on
The real clown as know is ideology

For Michael and Nick (Wherever They Are or End Up)

I love you so much, buddy and my thesis is and has always been I want people to have peace; I could definitely tell tonight that something was a bit off. But it'd be damn near impossible for you to ever alienate me, but I appreciate the follow-up. I'm really sorry you've had such a hard day, bud. A lot of people are having hard days right now. I struggle so much because I just want people to have peace, and that, for god fucking sake, includes you and Nick. I love you, man, and I never want the ugliness or the trauma of life or the bad of the world to turn you against your beautiful heart.

The Living's Legacy Is Love

I like cows. Cows eat grass and don't do much except graze and hook up with other cows. Humans, with their sentience and intelligence — both the greatest gift and the greatest danger ever conferred to life are constantly getting themselves out of problems they create by creating more problems for themselves, the world, and the cows. We are our best friends and our worst enemies. But I always maintain that love and goodness outweigh the badness. I wish people were more like cows. I love this world and believe it has no end. Eventually, I think what survives a person, the grave, etc, is what was in their heart. Choose love, grass, grazing, and peace. Like Sagan's pale blue dot, life ain't so shitty, and per Corso's comments, there is yet time to go back through life and expiate all that's been sadly done. Life is marvelous. Be like the cow.

A Riposte to the Upper-Echelon of the British Philosophical Aristocracy

"The universe may have a purpose, but nothing we know suggests that, if so, this purpose has any similarity to ours."

~ Bertrand Russell

"Ah, I disagree. If the universe's purpose weren't commensurate or hospitable to our purpose, Bertie, I don't believe we'd be around."

~ Alexej

Music is the Voice of God

If someone were born deaf and 80 or 90 years later, in the twilight of their lives, could somehow miraculously hear music for the first time afterward, I believe they could tell you the meaning of life.

Snowfall Takeout Girl

Have you ever been in Love?
Yes
No, I mean, like, had a wife? Something serious?
    Like true Love?
Yes, when I was 29
She was in the back parking lot outside my Kansas
    apartment building in late autumn
or early December.
I caught her on my way out and on her way into the
    apartment building
She had brought home her dinner — it was takeout
The snow fell softly
She glanced up at me, and our eyes met
She was mildly startled, but the smiles relieved, I think
I held the door open for her, and she thanked me a
    late-night
And?
That was it
Do you two get hitched or date or anything later on?
I don't believe I ever saw her again
No! It could've been so much more than that!
What! That's such a waste!
Hm….and yet it was beyond enough.

Eating Korean Pork & Kimchi & Rice at Christmas in the End Times

Slow-cooked pork with sodium-laden Gochujang sauce
White rice and ginger vegetable salad and dressings
Alcohols and Coca-Cola
Kimchi and avocado post-everything
No snow outside; there is not much snow anywhere
Some say the downfall of humanity, the world, and the times
A new dark ages;
Laughing, eating scrumptious food
Laughter is all that there ever was is or should, or could be
Stereo plays "New York, New York" by Sinatra
We are eating in New York at home for X-mas
And "Que Sera Sera"
We laugh, we eat, we rejoice
In the company, there is comfort and Love
The food is fucking delicious
We stuff ourselves
Drinking beer like water
Playing darts
Calm as can be and happier than happiest can be
The Christmas traditions continue uninterrupted
Got "Message" that Portuguese masterpiece for X-mas. Gift
    from Peter and Anna when
they were in Lisbon or wherever; now they're hitched. Dope.
The Philly Specials with Jason and Travis Kelce
And Springsteen plays back to back on the stereo
At full blast "Santa Claus is coming to town!";
Armstrong sings "What a Wonderful World."

And my thoughts EXACTLY

And nostalgic, N-O-S-T-A-L-G-I-C!

Photos of me as an 18-year-old; scraggly haired probably
about 210 lbs; total pothead

Then the classic:

"I DID IT MYYYY WAYYY!!!"

I swear to God, play that at my funeral many, many years
from now

The Sid Vicious version at the end of Goodfellas

Ah, what a grand life it is, indeed;

Some. Kinda. LIFE!!

Recounting an Interview with Neil deGrasse Tyson to a Sociologist

Yeah, I mean, I can make one unassailable comment on
     the notion of life after death.
Ha, what?
Your organs stop functioning, your blood oxygen drops,
     your body shuts down, you
lose consciousness, and then you expire.
Your temperature drops…to about room temperature,
     not cold, but lukewarmish.
After a few days, your body begins to decay
We are made of carbon, and what comes out of us is
     nitrogen
And whatever is left inside our bodies in the form of
     energy,
really just caloric energy, whirs off into the atmosphere
And then ideally, we are placed in a grave, and I like to
     think, as Keanu Reeves once
said, "…I think those who loved us will miss us."
That's not enough for some people, but for me, that's
     enough.
I don't think you're alone in thinking there, either, man.
Whatdya mean?
You sound just like every other compassionate atheist
     I know
I never said I was alone; I don't believe anyone is
     genuinely alone;
I don't even see from a mathematical or philosophical
     point of view how one could ever
indeed be alone; that doesn't even make any sense
SLAM!!

Sorry about your car door, man

So, man, super complicated philosophical problems just..
   not an issue, but closing a car door?

Uh…yeah, and keeping my pants on, and dressing, and
   finding a woman who can

tolerate me and holding a job, among many other really
   uhh.. irritating things, ha.

Nutshell from Jar of Flies

There is something so beautiful about Layne Staley and
　　Jerry Cantrell's work
Layne has always had the capacity to break me and heal
　　me all at once;
At their best, Alice in Chains kinda reminded me of
　　Conrad - swimming until they sank
　　　　it's not the same thing as drowning . . .
　The world is more beautiful because of songs
　　like Nutshell than it was prior to songs like Nutshell
It is the anthem of the unseen; the anthem of the hungry
　　ghosts
　Inside a workingman's realm of "dreams that could
　　have been"
Alice in Chains definitely saved me and likely so many
　　others in a myriad of ways;
　Probably the single, greatest band of the 1990's, too
　　often overlooked
Thank you Layne & Jerry - you both mean the world to
　　me;
　　　　I don't know what I'd do without you fellas in
　　this life
Thanks for writing the songs that needed to be written

A Dream Divested is Often a Dream Invested

I want to live in West Virginia.

I'm like a bohemian Paul Erdos, and I am Hungarian but
    not a mathematician per se;

Jose called me a communist, but a good communist; I'm
    not a communist; I'm more of

an eco-anarchist or a Colorado lefty.

My ideal living situation would be to be a boarder and be
    completely peripatetic, going

from place to place, lecturing, reading, studying, writing,
    and creating.

There is no actual endpoint, just the lifestyle and for the
    sheer joy of it all, ah!

You know what impresses me?

It's not Harvard-educated Ph.D.s - it's the single mom who
    achieves her bucket

list goal of completing her bachelor's from SNHU or
    DeVry on her dollar to create a

better life for herself and her child. That's so much more
    impressive to me than fancy

letters or elite schools.

I'm also encouraged by a man I met at a dropout recovery
    center when I was 19

He was 49 and was going back to complete his high school
    diploma; that is a genuine achievement.

Brand names do not impress me so much.

I find them dense and emotionally unintelligent and even
    vacuous and dull-witted

But what is it to believe?

Ahhhh, faith is not forlorn, and neither is believing in the power to transcend adversity,

    so do not reject or avoid it, but rather, conquer it, and

    then, in perhaps a rare hour —

CELEBRATE!

You have succeeded!

Do not be bashful; do not be prideful

Be bold, be courageous, and be authentically you

You are the only version of YOU

Any advantage you have in this life is being yourself

I still want to be that boarder as I have before in KCK

    and elsewhere

I don't need much

The less people have, the more they stand to profit

Be calm and be genuine, and thank you, and I love you

    too

P.S. - Exile on Main Street is one of my favorite albums;

    Keith Richards is super dope

on that L.P.

West Virginia, maybe briefly. I could hypothetically live

    with Harmony Korine or something, I don't know!

Between Friends

Life is always wonderful and nothing is wrong, right?
Yes, - or at least life is always beautiful but living can be
    difficult
        Right

But What About Nihilism, Doc?

I am a broken threnody for a God forsaking
post-Enlightenment world

From Balsam in Boulder 16 years Ago 2 "Later to RiRi" and a Conversation with Megan

I feel like life would be so unrewarding
        if it were all sunshine and rainbows

So after all, Armen dear friend, - Deadboy, like, without the
    rain there is no rainbow;

Megan ~ "Life is fucking weird"

Alexej ~ "I feel like that could be a good bumper sticker
    or something"

Starshine 2

There is a star that shines brighter than the rest
 far, far away and away away away
It burns bright and slow and long
It fuels itself eternity in and eternity out forever and ever
There is a star that burns brighter than all other stars
    anywhere
The star shines bright no matter what no matter when
 faithfully, eternally, lovingly
The cosmos is thankful to this star
And the solar systems are better for having such stars
    amongst them
Surely these bright bright stars are out there
They burn bright
They burn bright through the night and the eternal dusk
    and the eminent dawns
And keep everything fundamentally grand about the
    cosmos in good working order

Why?

Because we had to try

Glaucon, Revisited

And so, what makes me sad about machine learning and AI?
Is it the rapidly escalating global cold war and the AI arms
    race?
No, that's not technically new territory
But what about the factually unsophisticated truth that we
    are pouring billions into
making machines more clever than humans while we
    simultaneously continue to
defund public schools and communicate via emojis and
    memes?
While we become dumber, the machines become smarter
Well, then, I'm not an AI skeptic…literacy (not just
    psycholinguistically) but language is
so goddamn existential. I am proud to wear the appellation
    "Poeta", but I am grateful
and humbled and still thrilled to be a scientist of the word

Belief

If the ship were sinking, I would stay aboard, steady my hands, and play my violin.

/

Alexej Savreux was born in Burlington, Vermont, and grew up in the northeastern and southwestern U.S. Savreux is a longtime resident of both Kansas City, KS and Kansas City, MO. He owns and operates illogical conceits multimedia, a DIY media, and technological communications sole prop out of his apartment in Kansas City, MO. Savreux has served on the advisory board of Kansas City PBS, the artistic committees of NoDivideKC, and the Kansas City Electronic Music and Arts Alliance (KcEMA). His publications have appeared in periodicals as diverse as *Psychology Today, KC Studio, ScholarSpace,* and *The Pitch.* He is a 2016 Writer's Digest winner, a 2021 Shakespeare Prize Winner, and a 2022 recipient of an NEA Special Project Grant for the Centerpieces For Social Justice exhibit at InterUrban ArtHouse. He divides his time between Kansas City and New York.

This project was made possible, in part, by generous support from the Osage Arts Community.

Osage Arts Community provides temporary time, space and support for the creation of new artistic works in a retreat format, serving creative people of all kinds — visual artists, composers, poets, fiction and nonfiction writers. Located on a 152-acre farm in an isolated rural mountainside setting in Central Missouri and bordered by ¾ of a mile of the Gasconade River, OAC provides residencies to those working alone, as well as welcoming collaborative teams, offering living space and workspace in a country environment to emerging and mid-career artists. For more information, visit us at www.osageac.org

Osage Arts Community